Killing Germs

by Melanie Mitchell

Series consultants: Sonja Green, MD, and
Distinguished Professor Emerita Ann Nolte, PhD,
Department of Health Sciences, Illinois State University

Lerner Publications Company • Minneapolis

Lerner Publications Company
A division of Lerner Publishing Group
241 First Avenue North
Minneapolis, MN 55401 USA

Website address: www.lernerbooks.com

Words in **bold type** are explained in a glossary on page 31.

Library of Congress Cataloging-in-Publication Data

Mitchell, Melanie (Melanie S.)
        Killing Germs / by Melanie Mitchell.
            p.   cm. — (Pull ahead books)
        Includes index.
        ISBN-13: 978-0-8225-2450-2 (lib. bdg. : alk. paper)
        ISBN-10: 0-8225-2450-3 (lib. bdg. : alk. paper)
            1. Microbiology—Juvenile literature. 2. Medical
microbiology—Juvenile literature. 3. Sanitary microbiology—
Juvenile literature. I. Title. II. Series.
        QR57.M56 2006
        616.9'041—dc22   2004017911

Manufactured in the United States of America
1 2 3 4 5 6 – JR – 11 10 09 08 07 06

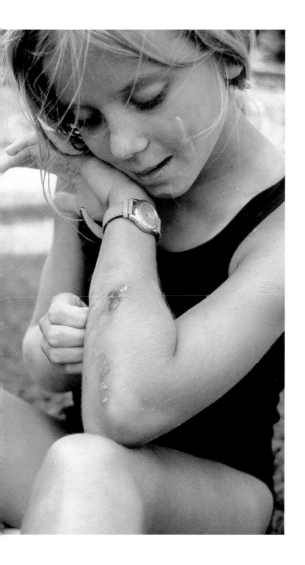

Look at the **scrape** on this girl's arm. What can you see?

It's not what you can see that's important. It's what you can't see. You can't see the **germs**.

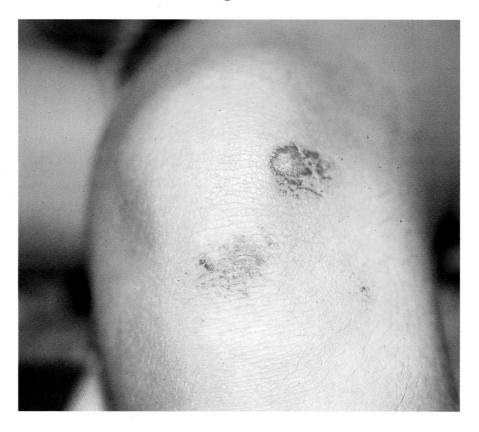

Germs are tiny living things. They can be seen only with a **microscope**.

Germs live everywhere. They live in the air. They live on the playground. They live in your home and in your school.

Germs live on your pet. And they live
on you. Germs live on just about
everything around you.

We touch many dirty things during the day. So lots of germs get on our hands. These germs try to get into our bodies.

Germs wait for you to touch your mouth, nose, or eyes. Germs can also get in through cuts and scrapes.

Germs that get into your body begin to **multiply**. Soon there are millions of germs! They attack your body. It tries to fight the germs.

Your body can kill most germs. Killing germs helps you stay **healthy**.

Your body cannot fight off all germs.
Sometimes germs make you sick.
They can make you sneeze and cough.
They can give you **fevers** and the flu.

Your doctor might give you some medicine to kill the germs called **bacteria.** Killing these germs helps you get well.

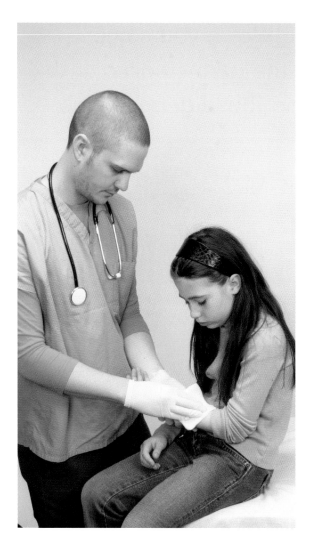

We can get rid of a lot of germs before they get in our bodies. Clean cuts and scrapes right away.

Then cover
them with
bandages.
That way,
germs cannot
get in your
body.

If you cough or sneeze, cover your mouth and nose with a tissue. This will stop germs from spreading into the air or onto your hands.

Washing your hands often during the day will kill lots of germs. Most germs cannot live in warm, soapy water.

Wash your hands after you go to the restroom.

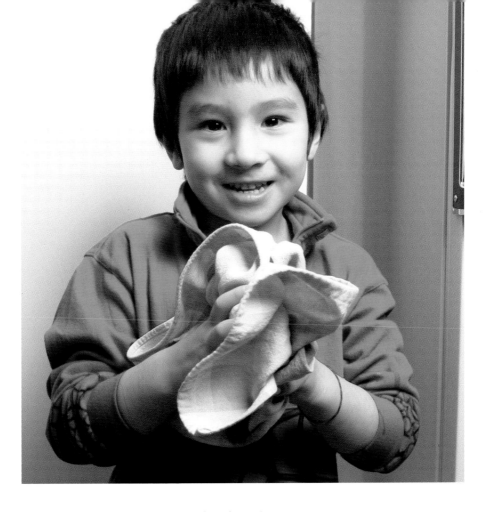

Wash your hands before you eat.
Don't forget to dry them off!

Wash fruits and vegetables before you eat them. This will kill many germs.

Look at this food. It has been sitting on the table all day. What do you think is growing on the food? Germs!

Always put food away as soon as you are finished with it. Make sure you tightly close bags and containers.

Another way to keep germs off food is to store it in the refrigerator. Most germs will die in cold places.

Remember to wash your dishes after
using them.

Don't drink out of the same cup that another person just drank from. Don't share forks and spoons that have been in your mouth.

Clean the counters and floors in your house. Use sponges, washcloths, and mops. Don't forget the soap or cleaner!

Germs live everywhere. You can keep most germs away. Keep your body clean. And don't give germs places to live.

Facts about Germs

■ Not all germs are bad. Our bodies need germs to help break down food. Germs are also used to make cheese and some medicines.

■ Antibiotics are medicines made in laboratories. When we are sick, these antibiotics can help us get well.

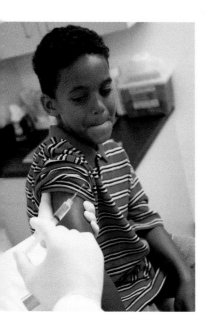

■ Antibiotics can only kill germs called bacteria. Bacteria can cause sore throats and earaches.

■ Colds and the flu are caused by germs called viruses. Antibiotics cannot kill viruses. Our bodies must fight off viruses by themselves.

■ Vaccines are shots made from a small amount of dead or weak germs. These germs help your body fight off some diseases before they can make you sick.

Your Body Strikes Back!

■ The best defense against germs is your own body! It has ways of getting rid of germs before they can make you sick.

■ Your skin keeps most germs out.

■ Small hairs in your nose catch the germs that you breathe in. Sneezing makes the germs come out.

■ People don't cry just because they are sad. Tears can wash away dirt, germs, and other things that get in your eyes.

■ Millions of germs live in your mouth. Your spit helps kill many of them.

■ Inside your body are special cells. They destroy the bad germs that get into your body. Without these cells, you would get sick all the time.

Books and Websites

Books

The Magic School Bus Inside Ralphie: A Book about Germs. New York: Scholastic Inc., 1995.

Nelson, Robin. *Staying Clean.* Minneapolis: Lerner Publications Company, 2006.

Nye, Bill, and Kathleen W. Zoehfeld. *Bill Nye the Science Guy's Great Big Book of Tiny Germs.* New York: Hyperion, 2005.

Ross, Tony. *Wash Your Hands!* Brooklyn, NY: Kane/Miller Book Publishers, 2000.

Websites

Germs, Germs Everywhere
http://library.thinkquest.org/J002353/

Kids' Talk
http://kidshealth.org/kid/talk/

NSF Scrub Club
http://www.scrubclub.org

Glossary

bacteria: germs that can cause sore throats and earaches

fevers: high body temperatures

germs: very small living things that can make people sick

healthy: fit and well

microscope: a tool that makes very small things appear bigger

multiply: to grow in number

scrape: scratches and small cuts on the very top of the skin

Index

Photo Acknowledgments

The photographs in this book appear courtesy of: © Beth Johnson/Independent Picture Service, cover; © Mark Clarke/Photo Researchers, Inc., p. 3; © SCF/Visuals Unlimited, p. 4; © Richard T. Nowitz/CORBIS, p. 5; PhotoDisc Royalty Free by Getty Images, pp. 6, 28; © Royalty-Free/CORBIS, pp. 7, 11; © age fotostock/SuperStock, p. 8; © Lisette Le Bon/SuperStock, p. 9; © D. Lovegrove/Photo Researchers, Inc., p. 10; © Image Source, pp. 12, 15, 17; © Tom & Dee Ann McCarthy/CORBIS, p. 13; © Todd Strand/Independent Picture Service, pp. 14, 21, 25, 26; © LWA-Stephen Welstead/CORBIS, p. 16; © Image Source/SuperStock, p. 18; © Brendan Curran/Independent Picture Service, pp. 19, 22; © Sucre Sale/SuperStock, p. 20; © Francisco Cruz/SuperStock, p. 23; © Norbert Schaefer/CORBIS, p. 24; © BAUMGARTNER OLIVIA/CORBIS SYGMA, p. 27.